WELCOM
CRICKET
LEGENDS

Lunar Press is a privately-run
publishing company that cares
greatly about its content's accuracy.

If you notice any inaccuracies or have
anything that you would like to
discuss in the book, then please email
us at
lunarpresspublishers@gmail.com.

Enjoy!

BIOGRAPHY

Born	24 April 1973
Nationality	Indian
Test Debut	15 November 1989
Final Test	14 November 2013

If anyone can challenge Sir Donald Bradman to the title of greatest batter of all time, then Sachin Tendulkar has to be in with a shout. He is the highest run-scorer in the history of both Test and One Day International (ODI) cricket, with over 15,000 and 18,000 runs, respectively. He is so loved in his native India that some people have labelled him one of the most worshipped sportspeople in history.

Sachin came along decades after Donald Bradman, but there were a lot of similarities in how they batted. Both were aggressive and loved nothing more than racking up colossal run totals every time they played.

Born on 24 April 1973 in Bombay (now Mumbai), Maharashtra, India, Sachin grew up with a lot of anger in him. His small size made him believe he had to start fights in school to show how tough he was, but he grew out of this phase later in life. His father was a poet and novelist, and his mother worked in insurance. Apart from the trouble he caused in his school years, Sachin was a hardworking kid.

Another similarity he shared with Donald Bradman was his love for tennis. Sachin was an exceptional tennis player, but his older brother steered him toward cricket. He felt that the calmness and conduct needed to play might help put Sachin in a better place mentally. It worked, and young Sachin was soon obsessed with being the greatest cricketer ever.

He quickly earned a name as a child prodigy*, with his skills being talked about throughout India. In a country that adores cricket as much as India, this is not an easy thing to do!

Surprisingly, Sachin spent his early teens wanting to be a fast bowler. He was good, but one of his coaches— former Australian player Dennis Lillee—convinced him to concentrate on batting. When Sachin won the Best Junior Cricketer award soon after, the decision to switch looked like a good one.

In 1988, at 15 years and 232 days, Sachin made his first-class debut for Bombay. The older players, faster bowlers, and added pressure should have gotten to him, but Sachin seemed to revel in it all. He scored 100 not out and became the youngest Indian player to score a century in first-class cricket.

He finished that 1988–89 season as Bombay's highest run-scorer.

Sachin followed that up by making his debut for India when he was still only 16. It was another record for him to break, and he became India's youngest-ever Test cricketer. Again, Sachin wasn't overwhelmed*, and within two years, he was smashing centuries for fun. Two of them came against Australia when Sachin had just turned 18, and the 148 and 114 he compiled made him one of the most admired young talents in the world.

His astonishing rise continued. In 1992, Sachin was the first overseas player to represent Yorkshire. He only played county cricket* sporadically*, but he still managed 1,070 runs over 16 matches.

When he was named captain of India at the age of 23, nobody questioned the decision. Sachin had become very mature for his age, shown in how he stepped into pressure situations like it was the most natural thing in the world. He led the team into the 1996 Cricket World Cup, and even though he was the tournament's top scorer with 523 runs, he couldn't help India past the semi-final stage.

By 1998, Sachin's popularity in India—and the world of cricket, really—had gone beyond stardom. He was mobbed everywhere he went, and it got even more intense when he was awarded the Rajiv Gandhi Khel Ratna award that same year. In India, this award is considered the highest possible honour that can be given to a sportsperson.

India came even closer to success in 2003, reaching the final of the World Cup. Again, Sachin was the top run-scorer (673) and Player of the Series, but India were beaten by a powerful Australian team in the final.

Sachin continued to be phenomenal throughout the following years. In 2005, he became the first player to amass 35 centuries in Test cricket, achieving it in only 125 Tests. Two days later, he broke more records when he was the first player to record 15,000 runs in ODI cricket. Then (take a breath!), two months after that, he became the first man to score a double century in a single innings of ODI play!

The comparisons with Sir Donald Bradman had been made long before these unbelievable few months in 2005, but after it, they were everywhere. Sachin's desire to score as many runs as possible was so like Bradman, making them both devastating batters. They never lost that hunger to be the best.

In 2011, Sachin finally won the prize he had wanted so badly. The 2011 Cricket World Cup was held in India, Sri Lanka and Bangladesh. Once again, Australia were one of the heavy favourites. But it was India's turn, and they beat Sri Lanka by six wickets in the final in Mumbai. It was the first time that a country had won the World Cup on home soil and the first time two Asian teams contested the final.

Sachin Tendulkar retired in 2013. Alongside Rahul Dravid, he formed the most prolific partnership in Test cricket. Together, they batted 6,920 runs for India and became so feared that many teams had already mentally lost before they stepped out on the field.

Since his retirement, Sachin has spent a lot of his time raising awareness for several diseases, and his work for UNICEF* has helped save many lives. He sponsors 200 children a year in India to give them a better life, and he is living proof that people can change: After a childhood spent trying to prove how tough he was, Sachin has become a tender, giving person.

GARFIELD SOBERS

SIR GARRY

CAREER STATISTICS

	TEST	ODI	FC	LA
MATCHES	93	1	383	95
RUNS SCORED	8,032	0	28,314	2,721
BATTING AVERAGE	57.78	0.00	54.87	38.32
BALLS BOWLED	21,599	63	70,789	4,387
WICKETS	235	1	1,043	109
BOWLING AVERAGE	34.03	31.00	27.74	21.95

Test = Test cricket, ODI = One Day International, FC = First-class cricket, LA = List A cricket

BIOGRAPHY	Born	28 July 1936
	Nationality	Barbadian/Australian
	Test Debut	30 March 1954
	Final Test	5 April 1974

Some players are considered good all-rounders, but not many truly are exceptional at batting, bowling and fielding like Garfield Sobers. He was one of the most incredible batters of all and enjoyed 20 years of bossing it in Test cricket for the West Indies in a career that spanned three decades. A true all-rounder and a cricketing legend.

Garfield Sobers was born on 28 July 1936 to Sharmont and Thelma and grew up on Walcott Avenue, Bridgetown, Barbados. After his birth, his parents found themselves instantly worrying about their son. They feared he would be teased in school and find it hard to fit in. Why? Because Garfield was born with 12 fingers.

What might be seen as a hindrance for some people became one of the things that made Garfield great. He used his extra digits to his advantage, gaining a better grip on the ball and bat and practising until his cricketing skills were superior to almost everyone. But Garfield didn't just excel in cricket as a child. He was a superb footballer and basketball player too.

Tragedy struck the Sobers's household when Garfield was only six. His father died fighting in World War II when his ship was torpedoed by a German U-boat*. Again, this is something that Garfield might have let hold him back, but he was strong and managed to get through it.

Alongside his brother, Gerald, also a talented cricketer,

they led their primary school to the Inter-School Cricket Championship three years running. By 13, several local adult cricket teams were chasing him. These included the Kent St Philip club and the Wanderers, who played in the Barbados Cricket League (BCL) and the Barbados Cricket Association (BCA), respectively. These were not part-time teams; they were the real deal!

His time playing against grown-ups was tough for a teen who was still growing, but Garfield revelled in the challenge. He practised twice as hard as everyone else, and when he was offered the chance to sign for a team in the BCL First Division, he took his chance.

Garfield Sobers made his first-class debut in 1953 at just 16. He batted pretty well, but it was his left-arm bowling that first caught the eye. He took 4 from 50 and 2 from 92 in his first attempts.

His whirlwind start to life in the top division slowed down for a while, and he wasn't called up for a first-class match again for another year. This time, it was against a touring Australian side, Melbourne Cricket Club, and Sobers played so well that he was selected for the West Indies team that was due to play England in the coming weeks.

Amazingly, Sobers's third first-class career outing was a Test match, and he had only turned 17. Now, how's that for pressure?

He didn't step out onto the field at Sabina Park in Jamaica until the fifth and final Test. Still, he bowled well, taking 4 from 75, including a wicket in his very first over. The West Indies lost a close-fought series, but

Garfield Sobers had been noticed!

Once again, his rapid rise stuttered a little. In his early years as a first-class cricketer, Sobers struggled to decide which was his best position. He was so good at all three that it was hard to pick.

A tour of England in 1957 put Sobers on the map. Many newspapers carried stories of the 21-year-old from Barbados who was dominating while batting, bowling and fielding. His form during the tour earned him a move to Radcliffe Cricket Club in the Central Lancashire Cricket League, where he played for five years.

Some of those years could have been better for Sobers in terms of his form. Many West Indian critics accused him of not fully living up to his potential when it came to international cricket. That changed as the 1950s became the 1960s, and over a 3-year period, he scored 2,250 runs in 24 Tests, maintaining a 93.75 average!

That run included his first Test century when he hit an unbeaten 365 against Pakistan. This mammoth total beat the previous record that had stood since 1938, but that wasn't the most amazing part. What really stood out was that he achieved it without hitting a single six. That meant that he was batting for a combined total of 614 minutes!

Garfield Sobers is still the youngest player (at 21) to break an individual Test record and be a triple-centurion.

His career exploded then. He was captain of the West Indies by 1965, instantly leading The Windies* to their first-ever Test victory over Australia, taking the new Frank Worrell Trophy* in the process. He followed this up in 1966 with a scoring total of 722 (103.14 average), 20 wickets and 10 catches against England in a Test series. His 722 included three centuries.

Sobers played his last Test match in 1974 at Queen's Park Oval against England. English fans packed the grounds as they scrambled to see the great man for the last time. As always, Garfield Sobers played with dignity and passion. He was knighted the following year.

Along with his staggering individual records, most ex-pros and fans agree that he is probably the greatest all-rounder ever to play the sport.

IMRAN KHAN

LION OF LAHORE

CAREER STATISTICS

	TEST	ODI	FC	LA
MATCHES	88	175	382	425
RUNS SCORED	3,807	3,709	17,771	10,100
BATTING AVERAGE	37.69	33.41	36.79	33.22
BALLS BOWLED	19,458	7,461	65,224	19,122
WICKETS	362	182	1287	507
BOWLING AVERAGE	22.81	26.61	22.32	22.31

BIOGRAPHY

Born	5 October 1952
Nationality	Pakistani
Test Debut	3 June 1971
Final Test	2 January 1992

Now we move on to a player who is not just a cricket legend but someone who was actually the Prime Minister of his native Pakistan for four years! Another all-rounder to add to our list, Imran Khan has always seemed like someone who could do anything he set his mind to. Outside of cricket, he has raised millions for charity and founded* many cancer hospitals.

Okay, we'll admit it: We are a little jealous of this guy's achievements!

Imran was born on 5 October 1952 in Lahore, Punjab, Pakistan. He was the only boy in a family with five children, meaning he probably never got to watch what he wanted on TV growing up, as he must have always been outvoted!

Joking aside, Imran was quite a shy child who struggled to come out of his shell. He received a good education, though, and attended the Royal Grammar School Worcester. This move to England in his early teens helped to break down the walls of his shyness somewhat.

Imran showed great potential in school, and not just in cricket. He was very intelligent and managed to get a scholarship to Oxford University. While there, he studied philosophy, politics and economics. The last two of these would come in handy when he became Prime Minister of Pakistan following his glamourous cricket career.

While still receiving his education, Imran made his first-class debut at the tender age of 16, playing in a match for Lahore. He continued to play for Oxford throughout this period.

Three years later, Imran had his breakthrough season. He made his county cricket debut, turning out for Worcester, and followed that up with his first Test match against England at Edgbaston. He was not even 20 yet!

It wasn't until 1974 that Imran started his ODI career. Once more, his debut came against England, this time at Trent Bridge. Imran stayed in England until 1976 to finish his education before moving back to Pakistan and nailing down his place as one of their best players.

It wasn't long before Imran Khan's name was getting mentioned in discussions about the most fearsome fast bowlers in the game. He soon began pioneering* the reverse swing bowling technique. It would be forever associated with him.

Imran's career continued to grow. By 1986, at the age of 30, he became Pakistan's full-time captain. In only his second Test as captain, he led Pakistan to their first win on English soil in 28 years! He also managed to do it at the legendary home of cricket—Lord's.

Pakistan's "firsts" continued over the next few years. Back in his home country, Khan captained the team to their maiden* Test series win and, soon after, their first Test series win over England.

A year later, Imran Khan retired from cricket.

Thankfully, this didn't last, and he was soon convinced by the then-President General of Pakistan, Zia-ul-Haq, to return to the national team. They knew that a side with Imran Khan in it was a lot stronger than one without!

When the 1992 Cricket World Cup began, Imran was 39. Still, he captained Pakistan and performed to his usual high standards. In the final against England, he felt that the team's batting lineup was weak. He promoted himself to the top order, playing alongside Javed Miandad. They batted heroically, and Khan had Richard Illingworth caught off his bowl to win the match. It was Imran Khan's last ODI match and the first time Pakistan ever won the World Cup!

In 1993, he continued his good form despite his older age. He recorded a Test bowling rating of 922 points against India, and his performance in this period still ranks third on the International Cricket Council All-Time Test Bowling Rankings. Imran is also the second-fastest player in history to achieve the all-rounder's triple (3,000 runs and 300 wickets) in Test cricket.

He finished his career as a cricketing hero in his homeland and the world over. His political career is also impressive, as we know from our introduction to him in the opening paragraph. Add that to his charity work and cancer hospitals, and we are looking at one astonishing human being!

IAN BOTHAM

BEEFY

CAREER STATISTICS

	TEST	ODI	FC	LA
MATCHES	102	116	402	470
RUNS SCORED	5,200	2,113	19,399	10,474
BATTING AVERAGE	33.54	23.21	33.97	29.50
BALLS BOWLED	21,815	6,271	63,547	22,899
WICKETS	383	145	1,172	612
BOWLING AVERAGE	28.40	28.54	27.22	24.94

Test = Test cricket, ODI = One Day International, FC = First-class cricket, LA = List A cricket

BIOGRAPHY

Born	24 November 1955
Nationality	English
Test Debut	28 July 1977
Final Test	18 June 1992

Now we have the only man who was faster than Imran Khan to an all-rounder's triple, Ian "Beefy" Botham. Beefy was an aggressive right-hand batter and a powerful fast bowler who dragged England through matches on his own at times. He will be forever known as a real character and someone who changed how people viewed the classic English cricketer.

Born in Heswall, Cheshire, on 24 November 1955, Ian grew up full of energy. He excelled in many sports, including football, and he might have become a full-time professional if cricket hadn't stolen his heart. In fact, Botham played 11 professional football matches for Scunthorpe United before his cricket career took off.

Ian's father, Leslie, fought in World War II, and the family moved to Yeovil when Ian was three. His parents claim that soon after the move, Ian became obsessed with cricket. He could be seen most days practising for hours on his own in the Botham's back garden, even from as young as 4.

His cricketing skills accelerated when he attended Milford Junior School in the early 1960s. The school's starting age for its team was 11, but Ian was so good that they asked him to play when he was 9. He would later say that playing against the bigger, more aggressive boys helped him become the tough player he was as an adult.

As well as running out for the Under-12s, Ian even

managed to get on the field for his father's team, Yeovil Cricket Club. He usually only played as a fielder, but again, the experience helped him mature quicker than most other kids his age.

If that wasn't enough cricket for him, he spent the rest of his spare time hanging around the Yeovil Cricket Club, hoping the team would be short a player and he could step in. Sometimes they were, and he had made several appearances for their second team before his teens.

In between all this, Ian continued to play football at a high level and was even offered a contract by then-First Division* side Crystal Palace. Ian had only just joined Somerset and was asked to choose between football and cricket. Thankfully for England, he picked cricket!

Ian still had two years of schooling to go when he decided to leave so he could give cricket his all. He was still only an apprentice at Somerset, so he asked to work on the ground staff at Lord's. This way, he could earn a few quid while also taking full advantage of the state-of-the-art equipment there!

His first-class debut came when Somerset played Sussex in 1972. Ian was only 17, but he was a big guy and seemed to fit right in. Still, it was a level he wasn't used to, and he was out after making only two runs. A spectacular diving catch later in the match impressed his coaches, though.

His second game was another defeat, but he claimed his first wicket, dismissing Geoff Howarth.

By 18, he was a regular for Somerset, and at 20, he was a

bona fide* star. In the 1976 season, he scored over 1,000 runs, got his first century, and earned his first England call-up. Now, that's what we call announcing yourself!

His debut for England was a big moment. He was the youngest player on the field and bowled admirably. That was until he came up against the great Viv Richards (who we will cover later!). Botham was brought back to reality with a bang, but it was all part of his learning. He now knew the standard he would have to reach to be one of the best.

The following year—1977—saw Ian make his Test debut in a match against Australia. He made an immediate impact, taking five wickets from 74, including one from Ian Chappell, his soon-to-be long-term rival.

Throughout his career, Botham's averages were always good but rarely great. Still, he had a knack for stepping up in the big moments, often taking wickets or smashing centuries just when his team needed it most.

The England captaincy always seemed destined to be taken by Botham, and he was given the honour in 1980. Unfortunately, his form dropped around this time, and England fell into a dark period of heavy losses. One of these more embarrassing performances came against Australia.

With England on the verge of losing going into the fourth Test, the pundits gave England zero chance of avoiding defeat. Botham clearly wasn't listening, as he smashed 149 not out to win the fourth Test, then dragged England to victory in the fifth. He scored 399 runs and took 34 wickets in the series!

For his charity work, which includes raising millions for childhood leukaemia research by walking from Land's End to John o' Groats, Ian is also a successful commentator for Sky Sports. He was given the title of Lord Ian Botham for both his cricketing achievements and his charity work, but we will always remember him for his aggressive cricket style and lovable character.

A true England legend.

SHANE WARNE

WARNIE

CAREER STATISTICS

	TEST	ODI	FC	LA
MATCHES	145	194	301	311
RUNS SCORED	3,154	1,018	6,919	1,879
BATTING AVERAGE	17.32	13.05	19.43	11.81
BALLS BOWLED	40,705	10,642	74,830	16,419
WICKETS	708	293	1,319	473
BOWLING AVERAGE	25.41	25.73	26.11	24.61

Test = Test cricket, ODI = One Day International, FC = First-class cricket, LA = List A cricket

BIOGRAPHY

Born	13 September 1969
Nationality	Australian
Test Debut	2 January 1992
Final Test	2 January 2007

One of the greatest bowlers who ever lived, Shane Warne, amassed a whopping 145 Test appearances in his time playing for Australia. He became a celebrity outside of the sport, too, and his face became recognisable to people who didn't even watch cricket. Some players perfect how certain things should be done in sports, but Shane Warne made them his own.

Shane Warne was born in Upper Ferntree Gully, Victoria, on 13 September 1969. His childhood was pretty regular, which is surprising given the flamboyant man he became. When we picture "Warnie" as a player, we remember the bleached blond hair, cool clothes and earrings, not a quiet kid going about his day!

His skills on the field during those childhood years didn't go unnoticed, though. He was offered a sports scholarship at Mentone Grammar in his teens, and he stayed there until he finished his education while playing cricket as much as possible. He also turned out for the University of Melbourne at times, playing for their Under-16s when he was just 14.

Warne's reinvention of the leg spin bowl and his near perfection of off spin bowling quickly brought him to the public's attention. People were talking about him as a future star long before he made his first-class debut.

After moving to St Kilda Cricket Club in the mid-80s, Warne began working his way up through the ranks. When he wasn't out on the cricket field taking wickets for fun, he was playing for St Kilda's Australian rules football Under-19s. It was said that he could have gone pro in either sport.

In 1991, Shane made the bold decision to move to England to test his skills in county cricket. He joined Accrington Cricket Club as their pro player, but he struggled early on due to the change in weather. His spin bowling needed to change for the softer surfaces, but such an adjustment takes time. Amazingly, Accrington didn't renew his contract, as they wanted their pro to excel in both bowling and batting.

His first-class debut came that same year for his hometown Victoria, and he later signed a bumper contract* with Hampshire Cricket Club, who saw the talent that everyone else apart from Accrington could see. While there, he scored his only two first-class centuries. But it was his bowling that was always his strongest asset.

After seven impressive performances for Australia's A team, Shane was selected for his first Test match. His debut came in 1992, but he and Australia were poor against India, and he was dropped for the fifth Test.

Shane Warne was a fighter, and he never gave up. He didn't let one disappointment stop him, and he buckled down and clawed his way back into the Test selectors' minds. A few months after his Test debut, he was back, putting in a dominant performance against Sri Lanka. In the second innings, he took the last three Sri Lankan wickets without conceding a run, winning the series for Australia.

Shane's breakthrough year came in 1993. In The Ashes

—his debut—Australia demolished the English, with Warnie taking 34 wickets in six Test matches. His first ball in the series, a devastating leg spin bowl, shocked the England team and everyone watching. From that moment, no cricket fan ever forgot the name Shane Warne!

He continued his form into the next Ashes, grabbing a match-winning 8 for 71 in the second innings of the first Test and a hat-trick (3 wickets in 3 balls) in the second. It was pure dominance from probably the world's best bowler in that period.

In 2000, Warne was named one of the Five Cricketers of the Century by Wisden Cricketers' Almanack*, and in 2004, he took his 500th wicket in Test cricket. He retired from Test cricket in 2007, having taken 708 career wickets (a record at the time), cementing his place as one of the most devastating bowlers in history. In fact, some would say the most devastating.

Sadly, Shane Warne was taken from us far too soon when he died of a heart attack in March of 2022. He was only 52.

His leg spin bowling, charisma*, talent, charity work, and everything he did to make cricket more popular will never be forgotten. Shane Warne is the true meaning of the words "sporting god."

VIV RICHARDS

MASTER BLASTER

CAREER STATISTICS

	TEST	ODI	FC	LA
MATCHES	121	187	507	500
RUNS SCORED	8,540	6,721	36,212	16,995
BATTING AVERAGE	50.23	47.00	49.40	41.96
BALLS BOWLED	5,170	5,644	23,226	12,214
WICKETS	32	118	223	290
BOWLING AVERAGE	61.37	35.83	45.15	30.59

Test = Test cricket, ODI = One Day International, FC = First-class cricket, LA = List A cricket

BIOGRAPHY

Born	7 March 1952
Nationality	Antiguan
Test Debut	22 November 1974
Final Test	8 August 1991

The man who earned the nickname the "Master Blaster" due to his powerful batting abilities wasn't just a devastating force in front of the stumps; he was also a part of the West Indies team that dominated throughout the mid-70s and early 1980s. He continues to work hard to promote cricket in the West Indies by trying to raise money for equipment and coaching at the grassroots level* while also promoting the sport in countries around the world.

Isaac Vivian Richards was born on 7 March 1952, in St John's, British Leeward Islands. He grew up in a family of cricketers. His father has played professionally for Antigua, while two of his brothers also represented the island at the amateur level.

After attending St John's Primary School as a kid, Viv moved to Antigua Grammar School on a scholarship. He was soon joined there by his younger brother Mervyn, who got in due to his cricket and football skills. Mervyn's talents in the latter* led to him making several professional appearances for the Antiguan national side!

With Viv's father being a top cricketer, he learned a lot growing up. As luck would have it, the Richards' next-door neighbour was also a pro, so Viv and his brothers had the best advice and training imaginable literally on their doorstep. As we have seen from Viv's later career, he took full advantage of this fantastic opportunity to learn and perfect his talents!

Still, his early career started quite slowly. At 18, Viv was only playing for a local pub team where he worked part-time for a little extra cash. The bar's owner loved to watch Viv play, and he pushed the young man onto bigger and better things through encouragement and time off to practise. He also supplied Viv with new whites, pads and gloves so he could continue to seriously pursue a professional career in cricket.

Viv knuckled down, and a year later, he made his first-class debut for a combined island team that included the Leeward Islands and Antigua. His performances that day and over the next few years brought him to the attention of Somerset's vice chairman, Len Creed. When Len asked Viv to move to England and play county cricket, Viv took a chance on himself. It would pay off in the end.

Viv didn't have to go on what must have been a scary adventure alone, as fellow islander Andy Roberts also moved, signing for Hampshire. Both men had been previously rejected by Sussex, who claimed neither had enough talent to make it in cricket!

Well, Sussex, all we can say to that is, "Oops!"

After quite a slow start to Viv's career, he suddenly became known in 1974 when he made an unbeaten 192 against a strong Indian side in the second Test of the series. This performance for the West Indies was so impressive that they quickly saw him as a strong opener from then on.

The following year was huge for the sport, with the creation of the first-ever Cricket World Cup. Viv's dominant performances alongside his talented teammates brought the trophy home for The Windies, and their period of dominance was just beginning! They beat Australia in the final by 17 runs, and the team was cheered on by the English crowd, who had enjoyed hosting the maiden World Cup and were happy to witness the West Indian style of cricket, which was fast and aggressive.

Viv later said that leading the West Indies to the 1975 Cricket World Cup was the best moment of his career.

His purple patch* continued through to 1976. Actually, that year is considered Viv's greatest by most cricket fans. He recorded 1,710 runs (a 90 average) that included 7 centuries, and all in only 11 Tests!

The 1979 Cricket World Cup was held in England once more, and it also saw The Windies winning the title again. This time they beat the home nation to lift the trophy, with Viv hitting a spectacular century in the final at Lord's.

Viv Richards became the West Indies captain in 1985, an honour he continued to fulfil until 1991. A year after becoming captain, he became the first player in history to hit a century and take five wickets in a single ODI match. This wasn't matched until 2005.

He retired from Test cricket in 1993 at the age of 41, having made his debut at 22. In that time, he compiled 121 Test matches, scoring 8,540 runs and 24 centuries. Apart from his dominance when batting, Viv was also a pretty handy off spin bowler who took 32 wickets in his Test career.

Viv Richards played in an era with some of the most

devastating fast bowlers in history, yet he always refused to wear a helmet. This is definitely a don't-try-this-at-home-kids thing to do! He was knighted in 1999 for his contribution to cricket and his charity work for the islands, and he wrote his autobiography a year later.

He continues to promote West Indian cricket and is a successful commentator. For the bowlers and fielders who came up against the Master Blaster, most, if not all of them, claim that Sir Viv Richards was the most fearsome batter they had ever faced.

RACHAEL HEYHOE FLINT

BARONESS HEYHOE FLINT

CAREER STATISTICS

	WTEST	WODI	WFC	WLA
MATCHES	22	23	51	43
RUNS SCORED	1,594	643	3,356	1,110
BATTING AVERAGE	45.54	58.45	46.61	42.69
BALLS BOWLED	402	18	870	64
WICKETS	3	1	7	5
BOWLING AVERAGE	68.00	20.00	66.42	7.80

WTest = Women's Test cricket, WODI = Women's One Day International, WFC = Women's First-class cricket, WLA = Women's List A cricket

BIOGRAPHY

Born	11 June 1939
Nationality	English
Test Debut	2 December 1960
Final Test	1 July 1979

Rachael Heyhoe Flint was a trailblazer in that she fought —and succeeded—to put women's cricket on the map. Her endless determination and supreme talent on the field helped pave the way for the thousands of female cricketers who followed. Without her, there might not be the same standard of TV coverage or high attendance figures.

Born on 11 June 1939 in Wolverhampton, England, Rachael grew up with a lot of sports in her life. Both of her parents were physical education (PE) teachers, and the school she attended, Wolverhampton Girls' High School (WGHS), had a good sports programme which she took full advantage of. After a few years at WGHS, Rachael's sporting ability was there for all to see. She was offered a scholarship at Dartford College of Physical Education, where she stayed until 1960.

Throughout her schooling, Rachael found herself most attracted to cricket, although she was superb at hockey too. She was a right-handed batter with immense power and was also very good at bowling, especially leg spin bowling.

Unfortunately, there weren't many opportunities in cricket for girls at the time when Rachael was coming through. Of course, her persistence would change all of that in the years that followed. Still, when she left school in the early 1960s looking to make a career in cricket, many people would have chuckled at her for being so gullible.

Thankfully, Rachael didn't give up on her dream, and in the end, she had the last laugh.

Another downside to the ignorance of the times was that women's Test cricket was hardly ever played, and it received little to no coverage. This meant that Rachael could only amass 22 Test matches between 1960 and 1979. That's just over one a year. In that time, Rachael managed to clock up a batting average of 45.54 in 38 innings. If women's cricket had been run like it is today, her numbers would surely have been much, much higher.

While hitting such unseen high numbers before that point, Rachael was also taking wickets, proving that her bowling ability was a force to be reckoned with too.

Her 179 in a single Test match was a world record that stood for many years, and the combined eight and a half hours she batted to record it was a show of the determination and passion that soon became her trademark.

As a batter, Rachael had the extraordinary—and extremely rare—ability to switch from aggressive, powerful batting to a more patient, opportunistic* approach. The reason this talent is so rare in players is that not many people can play full-on one minute and then calm and restrained the next. It was one of the things that made Rachael such a brilliant batter.

Only a couple of years into her career, Rachael broke down another barrier that had been holding women's cricket back. She became the first woman to hit a first-class six, which helped to show the doubters that the ladies could do everything that the men could. Rachael had a lot of these types of moments in her life, and all of them have been just as important as the next.

Her skills had also seen her named the captain of England in 1966, and she instantly led them to a six-series unbeaten run.

Rachael spent most of the 1960s trying to pressure the cricket bigwigs* into creating the Women's Cricket World Cup. At first, she was laughed at, but much like the people who sneered at her for wanting a career in cricket, she didn't listen. By 1973, her hard work had paid off.

Rachael captained her country into the brand new 1973 World Cup, and they were instantly seen as the favourites, mainly due to Rachael's immense talent. The event was held in her home nation, which only added to the romance of it all and proved that her hard work had been worth it. Any signs of an upset in the tournament were blown away in the final when Rachael smashed a half-century to see off the Australian challenge and win the big prize for England.

The World Cup was a massive success, and so many of the good things that have happened in the tournaments since would never have been made possible if it weren't for Rachael Heyhoe Flint. In fact, that World Cup in England came before the men's version had ever been held there, which is more evidence of the tireless work Rachael had put in to make it happen.

Three years after the success of the World Cup, Rachael became the first woman in history to captain a team at Lord's, leading England out against Australia at the 1976 Women's Ashes. Rachael gave up the captaincy two years later, and then in 1979, she retired from Test cricket altogether. Still, her legacy was firmly cemented by then.

She continued to play ODI and captained England at a World Cup once more in 1982. Sadly, her swansong* was disrupted by the old enemy, Australia, and England lost a close-fought final.

After the end of her playing career, Rachael achieved so much more. She worked on the Wolverhampton Football Club's board for many years, becoming their vice president in 2003. She wrote for many newspapers and became the first woman to host the popular World of Sport sports game show.

When Rachael became the first woman ever to be elected to the committee of the Marylebone Cricket Club and also the England and Wales Cricket Board, her work to bring the women's game to the public eye felt like it had been completed. She had started in women's cricket when there was barely a league to play in, and she built it from the bottom up. Without her hard work, women's cricket would still be left in the shadows.

Rachael passed away in 2017. She will be missed, but her spirit still lives through the high standard of cricket she helped to build.

BRIAN LARA

PRINCEY

CAREER STATISTICS

	TEST	ODI	FC	LA
MATCHES	131	299	261	429
RUNS SCORED	11,953	10,405	22,156	14,602
BATTING AVERAGE	52.88	40.48	51.88	39.67
BALLS BOWLED	60	49	514	130
WICKETS	–	4	4	5
BOWLING AVERAGE	–	15.25	104.00	29.80

Test = Test cricket, ODI = One Day International, FC = First-class cricket, LA = List A cricket

BIOGRAPHY

Born	2 May 1969
Nationality	Trinidadian
Test Debut	6 December 1990
Final Test	27 November 2006

The highest individual scorer in the history of first-class cricket, Brian Lara is a name and face that is known throughout cricket and beyond. His 400 not out in Test cricket is the stuff of legend, and the man known as "The Prince" became a global superstar in a sport that rarely produces people of such fame.

Unfortunately for Brian, his West Indies career happened at a time when The Windies weren't at their best. His skills and massive scoring helped to keep them competitive, but he missed out on a lot of team success due to this downturn in the West Indies' form. He came into the team just as the Viv Richards-inspired West Indies were starting to lose some of their dominance, but Brian Lara still left his mark on cricket in a way many others have never managed.

Born on 2 May 1969 in Santa Cruz, Trinidad and Tobago, Brian Lara was one of 11 kids. Money was tight, and his father Bunty and several of his sisters had to save in order to send Brian to the local Harvard Coaching Clinic once they saw his talent and love for cricket. He played every Sunday while there, and Brian later claimed that this was where he learned the fundamentals* of cricket.

His education was a bit scattered, and Brian went to a couple of different schools before settling at Fatima College when he was 14. Luckily, Fatima had an excellent cricket programme, and it wasn't long before his progress accelerated. In his first year there, he amassed 745 runs, maintaining an average of 126.16 runs per innings! His form earned him an early call-up to the Trinidad and Tobago Under-16s.

A year later, when Brian was only 15, he moved up to the Under-19s!

His rapid rise continued, and he had a massive year in 1987. At 17, Brian captained the Trinidad and Tobago youth team to the Youth Championship and scored a record 498 runs in the tournament. His star had risen, and now the world of cricket was waiting to see what Brian Lara could do when he started playing with the big boys!

They didn't have to wait long. Less than a year after captaining the youth team to glory, Brian made his first-class debut, playing for Trinidad and Tobago against the Leeward Islands. In his second match against Barbados, he scored 92 runs.

Brian became Trinidad's youngest-ever captain in 1990 when he was given the honour at only 20. That same year, he played his first Test match for the West Indies, impressing in the series against Pakistan. Despite his solid performances around this time, Brian still kind of went under the radar, but this was just because The Windies weren't doing very well.

His time of recognition would come. With the type of individual numbers Lara racked up, it was unavoidable!

By 1994, everybody involved in cricket knew the name Brian Lara. That year, he broke the two most sought-after individual records in the sport. In a Test match against England, he scored 375 runs, shattering the 36-

year record held by Garfield Sobers. Later that year, he smashed 501 not out for Warwickshire!

Despite these almost-superhuman efforts and batting miracles, Brian Lara often had periods where he underperformed. Some pundits and commentators questioned his dedication to the sport, while others pointed out that maintaining such high standards throughout a career was impossible.

Brian clearly didn't listen to his critics. In 2004, he broke his own Test record, batting 400 not out against England. The poor English must have wondered what they had done to annoy him, seeing as he always played so well against them!

Brian Lara's individual records would be too long to list here, and it would take a whole other book to fit them all in, from scoring 277 runs while making his first Test century to amassing 164 catches in his career despite being a batter by trade.

He retired from all forms of cricket in 2007, and even though he did attempt a couple of comebacks, he never reached the massive heights he had previously set. Brian continues to do a lot of charity work and does what he can to help the local Trinidad and Tobago communities. Some of the money he has raised has helped to expand the game throughout the islands.

He might never have reached the top of international cricket in terms of team medals, but his individual records are phenomenal. In truth, the fact that he scored so heavily and won what he did is made even more impressive when we consider that he did it in a struggling West Indies team. Only Sachin Tendulkar can compete with Brian Lara when it comes to batting dominance.

Mention cricket to somebody who doesn't follow it, and they will still have heard of Brian Lara. Mention the name Brian Lara to someone who loves cricket, and they will probably tell you he was the greatest!

JACQUES KALLIS

WOOGIE

CAREER STATISTICS

	TEST	ODI	FC	LA
MATCHES	166	328	257	424
RUNS SCORED	13,289	11,579	19,695	14,845
BATTING AVERAGE	55.37	44.36	54.10	43.53
BALLS BOWLED	20,232	10,750	29,033	13,673
WICKETS	292	273	427	351
BOWLING AVERAGE	32.65	31.79	31.69	30.68

Test = Test cricket, ODI = One Day International, FC = First-class cricket, LA = List A cricket

Born	16 October 1975
Nationality	South African
Test Debut	14 December 1995
Final Test	26 December 2013

This player was not only a world-class batter but a top bowler too. Jacques Kallis is the only cricketer in history to score over 10,000 runs and take over 250 wickets in both ODI and Test cricket. With individual records like that, we are clearly dealing with one seriously talented all-rounder!

Born on 16 October 1975 in Cape Town, South Africa, Jacques grew up adoring cricket. He was hitting balls as soon as he could hold a bat and practised a lot with his father, who he later said was a massive influence on his life. Jacques attended Wynberg Boys' High School and enjoyed nothing more than stepping out for their team whenever they played.

In 2009, Jacques returned to his old school as an adult, as they were naming their main oval after him. It still bears his name today.

He made his first-class debut at just 18 and continued his progress during a brief spell with Netherfield CC in England. In 14 matches for Netherfield, he recorded 791 runs, averaging 98.87 per game.

His Test debut came in 1993 when he was selected for South Africa against England. At 18, that amount of pressure was probably a little much, and Jacques struggled to compete against the stronger, quicker opponents of Test cricket.

The next few years were a time of growth. Jacques

practised hard, and by the time the 1996 Cricket World Cup rolled around, he was older and more competitive. Still, the South African selectors didn't feel he was quite ready, and he didn't play much cricket at the tournament.

His breakout season came the following year when he notched up 61 runs against Pakistan in a Test match. He continued his good run of form a few games later against Australia when his heroic performance rescued what had previously seemed like an impossible draw at the Melbourne Cricket Ground.

Jacques helped South Africa win the 1998 ICC Champions Trophy and was a regular for the team at the 1999 ICC Cricket World Cup. He won Player of the Series in South Africa's historic series victory over India in 2000, and by 2001, Jacques was the number one ranked all-rounder in the world.

The early 2000s were all about Jacques Kallis. In the 2003–04 season, he became the fourth player in history to make a century in five consecutive matches. A year later, he scored the fastest-ever half-century, hitting 50 off only 24 balls!

Kallis hit five centuries in a row again in 2007, this time in only four Tests. With his brilliant form came the South African captaincy, and he soon began to adjust his game to suit the role. His bowling became more important than ever as he took on more responsibility, but batting continued to be his strongest asset. By 2008, he was considered one of the best all-rounders to have ever played.

Kallis played his 150th Test match in the 2011–12

season. If people thought his skills might have faded after such a long career, they were wrong. His 150th Test saw him hitting his second double century, a fabulous 224. That Test saw him become only the sixth player in history and the first South African to achieve such an honour.

Since his retirement from playing, Kallis has coached at the highest level, including a stint as head coach of the Kolkata Knight Riders. He has also been a batting consultant for the South African and England national teams.

Jacques Kallis's charity work includes raising money for South African schools, among other important causes. He continues to sponsor girls and boys from many schools every year, paying for better education and opportunities while encouraging them to be the best version of themselves. Often, it takes someone who came from very little to see just how important it is to give back later in life. Jacques Kallis is clearly one of these special people.

Kallis's batting style has been called "safe" and "professional." He didn't have the aggressive batting style of players like Sachin Tendulkar or Brian Lara, but he did the fundamentals well and consistently. He is the type of player every nation wants in their team, and according to former England captain Michael Vaughan, Kallis was the greatest batter he ever faced.

It's not easy being an all-rounder, but Jacques Kallis did it with a style and grace that made it look easy. We think that's the greatest compliment we can give any sportsperson.

MAHENDRA SINGH DHONI

MAHI

CAREER STATISTICS

	TEST	ODI	T20I	T20
MATCHES	90	350	98	361
RUNS SCORED	4,876	10,773	1,617	7,167
BATTING AVERAGE	38.09	50.53	37.60	38.12
BALLS BOWLED	96	36	–	12
WICKETS	0	1	–	0
BOWLING AVERAGE	–	31.00	–	–

Test = Test cricket, ODI = One Day International, T20I = Twenty20 International, T20 = Twenty20

BIOGRAPHY	Born	7 July 1981
	Nationality	Indian
	Test Debut	2 December 2005
	Final Test	26 December 2014

Our first bona fide wicketkeeper on the list, the man known simply as MS Dhoni, was also a great batter. He won the first-ever ICC World Twenty20 with India and was also a Cricket World Cup winner, among other trophies. A born champion, MS Dhoni also captained the Chennai Super Kings to numerous Indian Premier League (IPL) titles. An Indian legend and a serial medal winner: There aren't many as good as MS Dhoni!

Mahendra Singh Dhoni was born on 7 July 1981 in Jharkhand, India. He was the youngest of three children, and his first love was football. He played as a goalkeeper for many years for his school teams, which helped in sharpening his wicket-keeping skills. It was one of his football coaches who saw how amazing Dhoni could be behind the stumps, and he convinced the promising kid to try out for the cricket team.

The rest, as they say, is history!

Dhoni's rise from that point onward was rapid. At 14, he was the starting wicketkeeper and occasional batter for the Commando Cricket Club, where he played from 1995 to 1998. Throughout this period, young Dhoni worked at the Kharagpur railway station so that he had some money to help his family pay the bills.

As sometimes happens, Dhoni found the step up to the men's game easier. Something about the speed of the bowling suited his batting, even though it was so much faster and more aggressive. The unorthodox* way that

Dhoni batted clicked with the faster balls. His stance worked almost like a moveable wall, and he used the bowler's own strength against him!

He made his debut for Bihar when he was only 18. By now, his batting had become his main asset, and he was already being talked about as a future Indian superstar. In the second innings of his first game, he made a half-century (68) and finished the season with 285 runs in 5 matches.

The 2000–01 season was seen as his breakout year. Dhoni started it well, recording his first-ever first-class century, and he managed to rack up five more half-centuries throughout the rest of the campaign. Despite his lower-order batting, Dhoni's hard-hitting style didn't go unnoticed. He was still seen as the man to lead India to glory, which was a role he loved.

The next couple of years were more than solid. Dhoni scored a 128 against Assam in the Ranji ODI tournament and was part of the East Zone* squad that won the 2003–04 Deodhar Trophy. His performances earned him a call-up to the India A team that toured Zimbabwe and Kenya the following year. MS Dhoni was well on his way to the top!

That tour proved to be a massive moment for Dhoni's career. In a match against a Zimbabwe XI, he produced miracles as a wicketkeeper, stumping* four players and making seven catches. He added back-to-back centuries during the tour to this already phenomenal performance.

His ODI career began in the 2004–05 season. This time, it was a tour of Bangladesh. Unlike the previous tour of

Zimbabwe and Kenya, Dhoni didn't start so well, and he was ran out for a duck* in his first innings. Luckily, his brilliant performances in the previous few years were enough to keep him in the team for the upcoming ODI series against Pakistan.

In the second match of that series—which was only Dhoni's fifth ODI international—he recorded 148 off just 123 deliveries. It was seen as his breakthrough moment, and it is still looked back on with fondness today. Dhoni was unreal that day.

It wasn't all centuries and stumpings for Dhoni during his glittering career. The 2007 Cricket World Cup was a disaster, and India crashed out in the group stage after defeats to Sri Lanka and Bangladesh. MS Dhoni needed to stand up and brush himself off, and that's precisely what he did.

Later that year, he was part of the Indian team that won the first-ever ICC World Twenty20. After the disappointment of performing so badly at the Cricket World Cup that March, winning the World Twenty20 was the perfect response.

The next two years were some of his best. Dhoni signed for the Chennai Super Kings in 2010 in what was then the largest contract ever given to a player in the IPL. He followed that up in 2011 by leading India to their second-ever Cricket World Cup, beating Sri Lanka in the final. Again, it was the best way to answer the critics who questioned India's quality after the previous World Cup.

Dhoni launched his very successful sportswear company, SEVEN, in 2016, and he owns a production company that makes some of India's top movies. He has a love for the Indian military, and he has donated money to help them over the years. In fact, he became a qualified paratrooper in his time away from cricket.

MS Dhoni retired from Test cricket in 2014 and all forms of international cricket in 2020. He continues to play—and dominate—in the IPL and won the fourth title for the Chennai Super Kings as recently as 2021. He gave up the captaincy in March of 2022, but it was handed back to him a month later!

To still be playing at the top level of cricket when he is 41 (at the time of writing this book) takes pure dedication and fitness. It would only take a look at MS Dhoni's trophy cabinet to know that he has that particular trait in spades. When will his cricketing story end? We can only guess, but let's hope he continues to boss it for another while yet!

MUTTIAH MURALITHARAN

MOTOR MOUTH

CAREER STATISTICS

	TEST	ODI	FC	LA
MATCHES	133	350	232	453
RUNS SCORED	1,256	674	2,192	945
BATTING AVERAGE	11.67	6.80	11.35	7.32
BALLS BOWLED	44,039	18,811	66,933	23,734
WICKETS	800	534	1,374	682
BOWLING AVERAGE	22.72	23.08	19.64	22.39

Test = Test cricket, ODI = One Day International, FC = First-class cricket, LA = List A cricket 59

BIOGRAPHY

Born	17 April 1972
Nationality	Sri Lankan
Test Debut	28 August 1992
Final Test	18 July 2010

Test cricket is generally seen as the highest level of the sport. It is where all the best players in the world give it their all. So, for someone to average six wickets per Test match, they have to be one of the best bowlers of all time. Muttiah Muralitharan achieved this and so much more. That is why he held the number one spot in the ICC player rankings for Test bowlers for 1,711 days straight, and it is why he was the first Sri Lankan player to be inducted into the ICC Cricket Hall of Fame.

Muttiah Muralitharan was born in Kandy, Sri Lanka, on 17 April 1972. If the name of his hometown, Kandy, wasn't already sweet enough, Muttiah's father also ran a successful biscuit factory! Muttiah was the oldest of four sons, and his passion for cricket was evident from a very early age.

His schooling wasn't easy, and Muttiah attended a strict school called St. Anthony's College, which was run by Benedictine monks*. Thankfully, their rigid rules didn't involve banning outdoor activities. St. Anthony's had quite a good cricket programme, and this was where Muttiah really fell in love with the game.

Muttiah was a solid all-rounder, batting in the middle order while continuing to take wickets with his unorthodox style of bowling. In his first two years at St. Anthony's, he took over 100 wickets and was named the best schoolboy of 1991. He stayed at St. Anthony's until he was 19 and signed for Tamil Union Cricket and Athletic Club almost as soon as he had finished.

He was also called up for the Sri Lanka A team that were touring England that same year, but he initially struggled against the more powerful players. He needed time to adapt, but claiming no wickets in his first five matches must have rattled his confidence. Still, the selectors had seen enough in previous games, and Muttiah was chosen again, this time for a Test series!

Muttiah made his Test debut in the second match of the series against Australia. His nerves didn't get the better of him this time, and he went on to claim three wickets from 141 balls. His style and power surprised his opponents, and Muttiah continued to grow into himself. Soon, he was one of the most feared bowlers of that era.

In the 1992–93 season, he bowled Sri Lanka to back-to-back Test victories over England and New Zealand. Muttiah didn't just perform well. He was Sri Lanka's sole wicket-taker in both Tests!

Muttiah's performances continued to amaze, but most of his Sri Lankan teammates weren't really up to his standard. As individual records fell, his list of team successes remained short. As if to prove this, Sri Lanka didn't get their first Test victory on foreign soil until 1995. Of course, Muralitharan led the charge as Sri Lanka recorded a 2–1 win against New Zealand.

In that series alone, Muttiah took 19 wickets, proving his doubters wrong. Some critics had claimed that his unorthodox bowling style wouldn't be effective outside of Sri Lanka. Maybe they should have waited a few years before making such snappy judgements!

Muttiah continued to improve his game over the

coming years. In the 1997–98 season, he broke several records. In 1997, he became the first Sri Lankan in history to reach 100 Test wickets, and the following year, he claimed his first 10-wicket haul*, bowling 12 for 117 against New Zealand in an 8-wicket victory. That same year, Muttiah claimed his career-best Test match figures (16 for 200) in a one-off Test against England.

The records continued to be broken, and in 2002, he became the youngest and fastest-ever player to reach 400 Test wickets. He did it in only his 72nd Test. Muttiah then went on to break his own record, becoming the fastest and youngest to reach 500 wickets, this time in his 87th Test.

To prove how impressive this is, it took the phenomenal Shane Warne 108 Tests to reach the same numbers!

Throughout his career, Muttiah was also a good lower-order batter, usually batting at No. 11. But it will be his dominant—and, yes, unorthodox—bowling that he will always be remembered for. When people told him his bowling style was all wrong, Muttiah Muralitharan must have just shrugged and said, "We'll see."

That is all we can ever do as human beings. There will always be someone telling us that what we are doing isn't right or good enough. When they do, just take a leaf out of Muttiah's book and ignore them. Believe in yourself, and you will prove them wrong in the end.

Muttiah Muralitharan retired from Test cricket in 2010, but not before getting the last 8 wickets he needed in his final match to reach 800 Test wickets!

His charity work has helped to raise money and awareness for education, mental health, hospitals and much more in Sri Lanka. In 2010, the International Cricket Stadium in Pallekele announced plans to name the ground after Muttiah in honour of his fantastic career.

Muttiah Muralitharan is still the player with the most wickets in Test cricket, and it could be a long time before his record is beaten. There are a lot of world-class bowlers on this list. Muttiah Muralitharan has to be the most dominant.

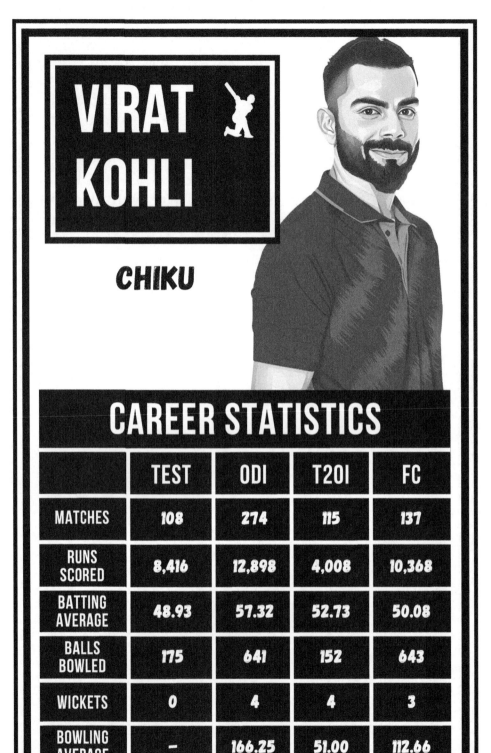

VIRAT KOHLI

CHIKU

CAREER STATISTICS

	TEST	ODI	T20I	FC
MATCHES	108	274	115	137
RUNS SCORED	8,416	12,898	4,008	10,368
BATTING AVERAGE	48.93	57.32	52.73	50.08
BALLS BOWLED	175	641	152	643
WICKETS	0	4	4	3
BOWLING AVERAGE	-	166.25	51.00	112.66

Test = Test cricket, ODI = One Day International, FC = First-class cricket,
T20I = Twenty20 International

BIOGRAPHY

Born	5 November 1988
Nationality	Indian
Test Debut	20 June 2011
Final Test	Still Playing

Another Cricket World Cup winner, Virat Kohli, was part of the Indian team that boasted other stars such as MS Dhoni, Sachin Tendulkar and Yuvraj Singh. He has the most runs in the history of both Twenty20 and the IPL, and in 2020, he was named Player of the Decade. Virat Kohli is India's most successful Test captain and a top-order batter like no other.

Virat Kohli was born on 5 November 1988 in New Delhi, India. When he was 3 years old, he picked up a bat for the first time and instantly asked his father to bowl to him. He has been smashing runs ever since!

In 1998, the newly formed West Delhi Cricket Academy began taking in the country's most promising talent in the hopes that they would be the next generation of superstar players. One of the first kids they signed up was 10-year-old Virat Kohli. According to his coaches at the academy, Virat instantly took to the more intense training, and his superior skills with a bat were there for all to see.

One of Virat's most important attributes wasn't just his natural skill, which he had plenty of. No, it was his dedication. It is said that he spent endless hours after training practising on his own. He was determined to be the best and knew that to get there, he had to work twice as hard as his most talented and determined competitors.

At just 14, Virat played for the Delhi Under-16s, and in

his first tournament with them, he finished as the competition's top run-scorer. These massive scoring numbers continued to grow, and the following year he scored 417 runs in just four matches for the Under-17s. That's an average of 117.5 runs per match!

Virat made his first-class debut in 2006 at 18, playing for Delhi against Tamil Nadu. He only scored 10 runs, but he showed his power and determination from the second he stood at the stumps. Virat also continued to play for the India Under-19s even after his first-class debut, and he impressed on a tour of England that same year.

Just when it looked like things were going perfectly, tragedy struck. Virat's father, who had been his hero and mentor growing up, died in 2006. Virat was only 18 and took it hard, although the people who saw him wouldn't have known it. In fact, he played for his local team the following day, scoring a 90 in the process.

Some people saw this as a heartless thing to do, but Virat knew that his father would have wanted him to play. It had been his dream to see his son play cricket at the highest level, and Virat surely wanted to honour him by doing just that.

By 2008, Virat Kohli was being mentioned as the perfect replacement for the ageing Sachin Tendulkar. As we know from our earlier biography, Sachin Tendulkar was seen almost as a god in India. It must have put terrible pressure on Virat to perform well, but he was up to the challenge.

Ironically, Virat's ODI debut came when he had to step in for Sachin Tendulkar after the legend picked up an injury. Virat was only 19 at the time, and he was quickly dismissed after only 12 runs. He picked himself up and, in the fourth match of the series, hit his first-ever ODI half-century.

From then on, Virat's scoring rapidly improved. The following year, he became only the third Indian player under 22 to score two centuries in Test cricket.

When the 2011 Cricket World Cup began, Virat was a regular for India. This was the tournament that was to be Sachin Tendulkar's swansong and the same Indian team that was captained by MS Dhoni. It couldn't have been a pleasant sight for the other teams when they stepped out next to an Indian team so full of current and future Hall of Famers!

Virat played every minute of India's triumphant World Cup campaign. He recorded an unbeaten 100 in the opening match against Bangladesh, making him the first Indian player to score a century on his World Cup debut. Against Sri Lanka in the final, he scored a solid 35 in an 83 runs partnership with Gautam Gambhir as India won the second World Cup in their history.

In 2013, Virat Kohli stepped into the spotlight that had just been vacated by Sachin Tendulkar following his retirement. Rather than shying away from the responsibility, he helped lead India to the ICC Champions Trophy that same year.

His romantic relationship with Bollywood superstar Anushka Sharma has only added to Virat's fame, and they are seen as the golden couple of India. Virat has spent many years promoting his vegetarian lifestyle, which has definitely worked for him, as he is considered one of the fittest cricketers in history.

He was still playing at the time this book was written, and his charity organisation, the Virat Kohli Foundation, continues to raise money for underprivileged children throughout India. He is already the record run-scorer in Twenty20 and the IPL, so who knows where his numbers will be by the time he retires!

BELINDA CLARK

CAREER STATISTICS

	WTEST	WODI	WT20I	WLA
MATCHES	15	118	1	244
RUNS SCORED	919	4,844	4	10,340
BATTING AVERAGE	45.95	47.49	4.00	49.47
BALLS BOWLED	78	90	–	648
WICKETS	1	3	–	18
BOWLING AVERAGE	28.00	17.00	–	21.33

BIOGRAPHY

Born	10 September 1970
Nationality	Australian
Test Debut	26 January 1991
Final Test	24 August 2005

Much like Rachael Heyhoe Flint, Belinda Clark has done a lot for women's cricket. She still holds several records, including the most runs in ODI (4,844), and she was the first woman to record a double century. When it comes to women's cricket, there haven't been many better than Belinda Clark.

Belinda was born on 10 September 1970 in New South Wales, Australia, to an amateur cricketer father and a state tennis champion mother. She showed real talent in a lot of different sports growing up, but it was always cricket that was her favourite.

Belinda attended Werris Creek Public School in her youth, where her father was also the principal. While there, she continued playing several different sports, including tennis, which she thought might be a better career option. Women's cricket was still a little behind the men's game in terms of financial backing in the 1970s.

She moved to Newcastle High School in her teens, a school that had an excellent cricket programme. It was around this time that Belinda started to see that a career in cricket might be the way to go after all. She was too good to walk away from it!

Her decision was made easier when she met Australian pro player Sally Griffiths. Sally took Belinda under her wing and drove her to Sydney on the weekends so she could play for Gordon District Cricket Club.

Her friendship with the older and more experienced Sally Griffiths helped Belinda to mature as a player. She knew she had to bide her time and the success she once thought impossible would come.

Belinda made her international cricket debut at 20 in an ODI match against New Zealand, opening the batting for Australia. She scored 36 in an eight-wicket victory, and her glittering career was well and truly underway.

Her Test debut came two weeks later against India. Belinda hit a century this time!

A terrible team performance from Australia at the 1993 Women's Cricket World Cup saw the selectors decide that big changes were needed. Some of the older players were moved out, and the young, aggressive batting style of Belinda Clark was seen as the way forward.

A new coach was brought in to help with Australia's transition. John Harmer decided to build the team around Belinda, and it was thought that her ferocious batting should be the way the rest of her teammates should play as well. It was a masterstroke, and a golden age of Australian cricket was born.

By 1997, Australia were superb. In February of that year, Belinda scored 131 runs from 97 balls in an ODI thumping of Pakistan, then led Australia to victory over New Zealand in the Rose Bowl series. Belinda calls this performance the greatest of her career. It's hard to argue with her point, and anyone who watches footage of that series would find it hard to disagree.

Her record-breaking double century came later that year and at the 1997 World Cup of all places! Australia went on to win the whole tournament, beating New Zealand once more in the final. Belinda finished the year with 970 runs, which is still a record.

With Belinda Clark as captain, Australia continued their dominant run. There was a blip in 2001 when they lost a close final to the old enemy New Zealand, but they bounced back later that year when they beat England in The Ashes.

Australia regrouped for the 2005 World Cup, and Belinda led them to their second title in eight years. Her dominant performance against England in the semi-final was unbelievable, and her batting throughout the tournament cemented her place as one of the greatest of all time.

Belinda Clark's international career came to an end that same year. She played her last Test match against England in The Ashes and then wrapped up her ODI career against the same team. The latter of these was her 118th ODI appearance!

Since her retirement, Belinda has spent a lot of her time continuing her work to promote women's cricket. Her efforts have helped to raise money for just that cause, and she is someone that the game of cricket holds dear to its heart. Without people like Belinda Clark, Rachael Heyhoe Flint and Mithali Raj (we'll get to her very shortly), women's cricket would be in a much worse state.

ALASTAIR COOK

CAPTAIN COOK

CAREER STATISTICS

	TEST	ODI	FC	LA
MATCHES	161	92	338	178
RUNS SCORED	12,472	3,204	25,807	6,510
BATTING AVERAGE	45.35	36.40	47.00	39.93
BALLS BOWLED	18	–	294	18
WICKETS	1	–	7	0
BOWLING AVERAGE	7.00	–	32.00	–

Test = Test cricket, ODI = One Day International, FC = First-class cricket, LA = List A cricket

BIOGRAPHY

Born	25 December 1984
Nationality	English
Test Debut	1 March 2006
Final Test	7 September 2018

Opening batter, second-most-capped English player in history, cricketing legend, talented musician—there isn't much Mr Cook can't do! A left-handed batter who recorded 33 Test centuries, Sir Alastair is a true English living hero.

One of the younger people on this list, Alastair was born in Gloucester, England, on 25 December 1984. When he came into the world that Christmas Day, we wonder if one of his parents had asked Santa for a cricketing legend as a present!

Alastair's mother was a teacher, and his father was a telecommunications engineer who adored cricket. When Alastair started showing an early interest in it, his father encouraged him. But it wasn't just sporting that young Alastair excelled in—he was an extremely talented musician who had mastered the clarinet by the time he was 8!

Growing up in Essex, Alastair attended St Paul's Cathedral School in London. Along with playing cricket there, he also spent long summers at the Maldon Cricket Club, where he continued his growth as a player. In fact, by the time he was 11, Alastair had already made a couple of appearances for the adult's Third XI. Think about that for a minute: The kid was just 11, and he was batting against the men!

By the end of his time at St Paul's, most people already suspected that Alastair would be playing first-class cricket sooner rather than later. In his final year at St Paul's, he averaged 168 runs per match.

Alastair later moved on to Bedford School, as they had one of the best music programmes in the country while also having a great cricket team. While there, he learned how to play the piano, and he continued his clarinet lessons and sang in the school's band. During his time at Bedford, everything changed for Alastair when the Marylebone Cricket Club (MCC) showed up for a practice game.

MCC were a player short, and they asked Alastair to switch teams and play for them. He agreed, and he smashed a century in his first innings. From that point on, cricket overtook music as Alastair's main interest.

Even though he was one of the younger players at Bedford, Alastair became their main batter after that. Over the next four years, he hit 17 centuries and was Bedford's captain by his final year. He was also president of the Music Society.

In that final year as captain, Alastair scored 1,287 runs with an average of 168.87 runs per match, which is still the school's record. He left Bedford with a career in cricket almost guaranteed, but he never let the pressure distract him. In fact, his final grades were some of the best in the county.

At 16, he became a part of the Essex academy. He made his first-class debut for them against Nottinghamshire County Cricket Club in 2003, making a catch and scoring 13 runs in his first innings. In the second innings, he scored 69 not out and helped a struggling Essex team to a 9-wicket victory.

Essex had already confirmed their relegation that year just as Alastair was breaking into the team, so they needed a new hero to help raise their fans' morale. Alastair was the perfect fit, and he had secured his place as an opener before he turned 18. He scored his first first-class century in 2004 (128), and by 2005, he had made his Ashes debut.

A few days before that proud Ashes moment, he had another one when he was named the 2005 Professional Cricketers' Association Young Cricketer of the Year.

By 2006, Alastair was a regular in the England team—playing in all formats—so his county cricket appearances became less frequent. Still, when he did play for Essex, he was superb, and he averaged 141.3 per match! These numbers dropped in 2007, as his attention and time fell more on his international career.

In his first Test series in 2006 against India, he smashed 60 and 104 in his first and second innings. What makes this amazing performance even more impressive is that Alastair had only been brought into the team after several injuries to other players. He had only arrived in India a couple of days before he stepped out onto the crease!

That first year in Test cricket was superb for Alastair on an individual level. He scored over 1,000 runs, including centuries against Bangladesh, India, Pakistan and Sri Lanka. By the time he was in his early twenties, he had scored more runs or centuries than any English player had so young.

After starring in the 2009 Ashes, he deputised as Test captain in 2010. That same year, he was named

England's full-time ODI captain. He helped England retain The Ashes in 2011 and was named full-time Test captain in 2012. That must have been a crazy three years for the young man!

Soon after being named Test captain, Alastair led England to their first Test series victory in India for almost 30 years. During that tour, he also became the first player to record centuries in his first five Tests as a captain.

He passed Graham Gooch's 8,900 Test runs record in 2015 and stepped down as Test captain the following year. He continued to play Test cricket, though, and in 2018, he broke another record when he competed in his 153rd Test match in a row. Much like Virat Kohli, Alastair Cook has always kept himself in superb shape, which is why he has been able to maintain his fitness for so long.

Alastair Cook retired from international cricket in 2018 but continues to play for Essex. He scored his 70th first-class century in April 2022.

Away from cricket, Alastair donates a lot of his time and money to many different charities and causes. He continues to practise music, and his saxophone skills have been used in the children's TV show Freefonix! He also runs his own farm in Leighton Buzzard.

England has produced some fantastic batters throughout history. As far as the modern batter goes, are there many better than Sir Alastair Cook?

JACK HOBBS

THE MASTER

CAREER STATISTICS

	TEST	FC
MATCHES	61	834
RUNS SCORED	5,410	61,760
BATTING AVERAGE	56.94	50.70
BALLS BOWLED	376	5,217
WICKETS	1	108
BOWLING AVERAGE	165.00	25.03

Test = Test cricket, FC = First-class cricket

BIOGRAPHY

Born	16 December 1882
Nationality	English
Test Debut	1 January 1908
Final Test	16 August 1930

Another opening batter like Alastair Cook, Jack Hobbs was someone who liked to hit the big numbers too. The only difference between him and Alastair is that Jack came along around 100 years beforehand! He is still the highest-scoring century-maker in first-class cricket history. The man nicknamed "The Master" was also an exceptional fielder and a very good right-arm medium-pace bowler. All of this is surely why he was the first cricketer to ever be knighted!

Jack Hobbs was born on 16 December 1882 in Cambridge, England. He was the eldest of 12 children and grew up in poverty, playing cricket on the streets near his home. He attended York Street Boys' School, where Jack later admitted that he struggled with his schoolwork but always performed brilliantly in sports.

During the weekends and after school, Jack had to work for a wealthy local family for a small wage in order to help his family with the bills. He left school in his teens and began working with his father as a gas fitter while playing cricket as much as possible in his spare time.

In this period, Jack played a lot of cricket around Cambridge, but he wasn't seen as someone who could make it at the first-class level. A lot of discrimination was involved in creating this view, as cricket was seen as a wealthy man's sport in the late 19th and early 20th centuries and not something that the less fortunate should be playing.

By the time Jack was 19, his batting had improved drastically. He scored his first century—a 102 for Ainsworth against Cambridge Liberals—but the rest of that 1901–02 season was pretty average. He was still learning, but it wouldn't take long until he was scoring centuries for fun.

Jack Hobbs turned professional in 1902, signing for his local team, Cambridge. He quickly began hitting centuries, and his high scoring and aggressive batting style made him a bit of a local celebrity. The way Jack was playing cricket had never been seen before. He was revolutionising the sport and didn't even know it, but some of the older players didn't like his flash style.

His rapid rise was interrupted when his father died suddenly in 1903. With the Hobbs family struggling for money, Jack was forced to go back to work, which cut down his playing time for Cambridge. Pro cricket legend and Surrey star Tom Hayward saw real potential in Jack, and he helped out financially as much as he could. He also got Jack a trial with Surrey, who could pay enough for Jack to support his family and concentrate solely on cricket.

Jack impressed during his trials and earned his contract with Surrey, and by 1905, he was batting alongside his hero Tom Hayward for them.

He made his first-class debut for Surrey that year, hitting 18 runs in his first innings and then a quick-fire 88 in his second. In his next match against Essex, he scored his maiden first-class century (155). Jack hit a few more centuries that season, but the sheer volume of games was new to him, and it affected his fitness.

Jack spent the winter months training hard and returned for the next campaign in much better shape. His consistency improved alongside his fitness, and he was soon dominating and high scoring just about every time he played. Jack hit several centuries, including another one against Essex, who had rejected him in his youth!

Jack's partnership with Tom Hayward was devastating. It lasted until 1914, but Jack sometimes played with major butterflies in his stomach due to him being so intimidated by his older, more famous teammate. In fact, Jack was so nervous around Tom that he couldn't even build up the nerve to ask him to his wedding!

The start of Jack's Test career didn't come until the 1907–08 season, even though he was probably the best batter in the world at the time. England's captain, Arthur Jones, didn't like him, and he thought the way Jack played was too aggressive.

As much as Arthur Jones tried to hold Jack back, the people knew what they wanted and demanded that Jack play. He made his Test debut in 1908 at the Melbourne Cricket Ground, opening the batting on the second day and recording 83 runs in 181 minutes. Even the team's captain couldn't drop him after that, and Jack kept his place for the rest of the series.

From then on, Jack's knack for hitting centuries really took off. It is said that he sometimes stopped at 100 just so his teammates could have a chance to play!

World War I (1914–18) interrupted his career, and Jack served in the Royal Flying Corps throughout the conflict. By the time cricket resumed in 1919, Jack was

37. With some of his physical power gone, he adjusted his game accordingly. He became more calm, collected, shrewd and cunning in his batting. He played hard in patches of the game, then slowed it down to regenerate when he could.

Amazingly, Jack scored higher than ever while in his early forties, and between the age of 43 and 46, he scored over 11,000 runs.

One of the things that Jack Hobbs did that no one else had done before him was to become a global cricket star. Before 1925, such a thing was unheard of in cricket, or any sport for that matter. Jack starred in adverts and made public appearances all over the world. When he scored 221 against a touring West Indies team at the age of 50, it was global news.

In February of 1935, Jack Hobbs finally announced his retirement at the grand old age of 53. He wrote several books on cricket and a couple of autobiographies, all while running his sports shop well into his old age.

Jack Hobbs became the first cricketer to be knighted in 1953 and passed away in 1963. He might have spent the early part of his career in awe of Tom Hayward, but Sir Jack Hobbs soon surpassed his hero to become the original cricket superstar. Without him, cricket would have taken a lot longer to reach the popularity we see today.

W.G. GRACE

THE DOCTOR

CAREER STATISTICS

	TEST	FC
MATCHES	22	870
RUNS SCORED	1,098	54,211
BATTING AVERAGE	32.29	39.45
BALLS BOWLED	666	124,833
WICKETS	9	2,809
BOWLING AVERAGE	26.22	18.14

Test = Test cricket, FC = First-class cricket

BIOGRAPHY

Born	18 July 1848
Nationality	English
Test Debut	6 September 1880
Final Test	1 June 1899

Now we move from Sir Jack Hobbs, who played cricket until he was 53, to W.G. Grace, who did so until he was 66. Yep, you read that right: W.G. Grace played cricket until he was 66 years old! As well as that, he came along even earlier than Jack Hobbs, having made his first-class debut in 1865. But W.G. Grace's contribution to cricket goes so much deeper than that. He changed the way people saw the game almost totally. Without him, there really wouldn't be such a thing as high-scoring cricket or even a place in the game for Jack Hobbs himself.

William Gilbert Grace, or just simply W.G. Grace, was born in Downsend, England, on 18 July 1843. His father was a doctor, and the Graces were considered an average Victorian* family. After a very serious case of pneumonia when he was a child, William's father decided that it might be best if he was homeschooled. William's illness had left him weak and frail for a long time afterwards.

As William hit his teens, his strength started to return. He suddenly had energy he hadn't had in years and needed to burn it. He found the perfect way to do this when he discovered cricket and quickly realised that he was a fantastic all-rounder.

Cricket was a little more scattered in the mid-19th century, and there weren't as many leagues and organisations, especially for youngsters. Still, William managed to make his first-class debut at the age of 15, and the following ten years are often considered the most important in the history of cricket. New rules such as over-arm bowling being allowed (Yep, there was a time when you had to bowl underarm!) were fundamental in making cricket more popular.

In his late teens, William was approached by both Oxford University Cricket Club and Cambridge, but his father made him turn them down. He wanted his son to go to medical school as he had, and he believed that cricket wasn't a real career. Before W.G. Grace, it kind of wasn't!

William enrolled in Bristol Medical School just before his 20th birthday, but by then, he was already being called the best cricketer in the world. Only a couple of days after he turned 18, William had scored 224 not out in one innings for an England XI versus Surrey match at the Oval. He would have scored more but left midway to compete in and win a hurdles event that was taking place close by.

W.G. Grace had one of his best years in cricket in 1871. In total, he amassed 2,739 runs, which was the first time anyone had ever scored more than 2,000 in a single year. This included 10 centuries and a 268 at the Oval once again.

Throughout his cricket career, he continued to practise medicine, running a busy doctor's office in his hometown. On top of that, he played football for the Wanderers*, loved lawn bowls, ran hurdles, and played golf. We guess W.G. Grace liked to keep busy!

He became the first player in history to do a double of 1,000 runs and 100 wickets in a season in 1873, then went on to repeat that amazing achievement eight times in a row!

Test cricket didn't really take off until 1877, and W.G. Grace was already 28 by then. He didn't make his Test debut for another three years and quickly scored England's first-ever Test century in a match against Australia. The next 22 Tests he competed in were all against the same opposition, and William continued playing Tests until he was 50.

A lot of W.G. Grace's scoring records have been broken over time, as he played so much amateur cricket in between first-class and Test cricket. This was simply because there was more money in amateur cricket. Players were given one-off payments by wealthy businessmen who wanted to host cricketing events on their private grounds or at the Oval, and W.G. Grace was the Lionel Messi or Cristiano Ronaldo of cricket at the time, so he was the big ticket!

W.G. Grace continued playing amateur cricket until he was 66. Even then, he finished his last innings with a 69 not out!

He died a year after his final game. It said that his death rocked Britain as much as Winston Churchill's fifty years later. Now, that's saying something.

MITHALI RAJ

CAPTAIN COOL

CAREER STATISTICS

	WTEST	WODI	WT20I
MATCHES	12	232	89
RUNS SCORED	699	7,805	2,364
BATTING AVERAGE	43.68	50.68	37.52
BALLS BOWLED	72	171	6
WICKETS	0	8	0
BOWLING AVERAGE	–	11.37	–

BIOGRAPHY

Born	3 December 1982
Nationality	Indian
Test Debut	14 January 2002
Final Test	30 September 2021

As the highest run-scorer in the history of women's international cricket, Mithali Raj deserves her place on any list of great sportspeople. She is also the only cricketer to surpass 7,000 runs in Women's ODI and the first to score seven consecutive half-centuries in the same format. Mithali has smashed lots more records—far too many to squeeze in here!

Mithali Raj was born in Jodhpur, Rajasthan, India, on 3 December 1982. Her father was in the Indian Air Force and was away a lot, but Mithali found comfort in cricket. She watched as much as she could on TV, and by the age of 10, her talents had become known around the neighbourhood and beyond.

When she started at Keyes High in her teens, her talent blossomed even more. Now that she was surrounded by other good players and stronger bowlers, Mithali's batting improved greatly. She was soon on her way to becoming the devastating top-order batter we know her as today.

Her growing reputation as a serious batter had much to do with Mithali's range. Her swift, dancer-like footwork confused bowlers, and she was able to change to a more powerful batting stance in a millisecond. It was a perfect combination and one that she used to dominate the sport for years to come.

Mithali's talents didn't go unnoticed, and she was fast-tracked* into the Indian international setup. Her ODI debut came when she was barely 16, but if the pressure got to her, she didn't show it. Mithali hit an unbeaten 114.

Soon, Mithali was India's star player and first-order batter. At 19, she broke the record for the highest Test score (214) against England. The following year, she was given the Arjuna Award, which is the second-most prestigious* award that can be given to a sportsperson in India.

India's fortunes improved with Mithali's rise in dominance. She led them to their first-ever World Cup final in 2005, but India just missed out to Australia, who had the excellent Belinda Clark and Cathryn Fitzpatrick (we cover her next!) among others in their team. Mithali didn't let the disappointment hold her back, and in 2006, she helped India record their maiden Test series victory over England.

With her batting already near perfection, Mithali continued to hone her bowling skills. She never got them to the level of her batting, but they were good enough to make her a fearsome leg-break bowler all the same. Did she feel like she needed to do everything if India were to succeed? Who knows, but she made India a much better team wherever she played.

Mithali was India's captain for the 2013 World Cup, which was being held in her home country for the first time since 1978. It was a proud moment for her, but India performed poorly, finishing bottom of their group.

On a personal level, Mithali was still performing exceptionally. The same year as India's World Cup disappointment, she was the No. 1 cricketer on the ODI chart. Such individual rewards wouldn't have meant much to a winner like Mithali, who must have craved a World Cup medal with her team more than anything, but it still shows the ridiculous standards she continued to set.

The next World Cup in England brought more disappointment, this time with another loss in the final to the host nation. India and Mithali had been superb throughout, but victory proved just one step too far in the end.

Mithali became the first woman to complete two decades of ODI cricket in 2019 and continued to play for another three years before she retired. She still holds many of the most impressive individual records in women's cricket, and she is a national celebrity in India.

In 2022, a movie was made about her life called Shabaash Mithu. The film didn't do very well, but just the idea of a movie being made about the life of a female sportsperson in India was a big step forward for equality in sports. It shows just how much the game and the world's view have changed for the better.

Mithali Raj was the type of aggressive, high-scoring batter that made people get up off their seats. Players like her are the reason people love cricket, and the heights she carried India to might never be seen again in our lifetime. Mithali is a genuine sporting legend and a top-order batter to rival anyone.

RICKY PONTING

PUNTER

CAREER STATISTICS

	TEST	ODI	FC	LA
MATCHES	168	375	289	456
RUNS SCORED	13,378	13,704	24,150	16,363
BATTING AVERAGE	51.85	42.03	55.90	41.74
BALLS BOWLED	575	150	1,506	349
WICKETS	5	3	14	8
BOWLING AVERAGE	54.60	34.66	58.07	33.62

Test = Test cricket, ODI = One Day International, FC = First-class cricket, LA = List A cricket

BIOGRAPHY

Born	19 December 1974
Nationality	Australian
Test Debut	8 December 1995
Final Test	3 December 2012

Here is someone who played—and starred—for Australia during their most recent Golden Era. Ricky Ponting is the most successful captain for any nation in international cricket, having won 220 of his 324 matches. A batter with a fierce stroke and winning mentality, he was voted the Cricketer of the Decade 2000!

Like quite a few of the people on this list, Ricky grew up surrounded by cricket. His mother was a great player, and his father was an amateur cricketer who played in between a semi-professional Australian Rules Football career. Also, Ricky's uncle Greg played Test cricket for Australia! So, when Ricky was born on 19 December 1974, it might have been thought that his destiny was already written in the stars.

Ricky grew up in Tasmania, Australia, in an otherwise working-class family. He took to cricket right off the bat (nice pun, huh!) and was playing for a very good Mowbray Under-13s when he was just 11. A year later, during a five-day tour of Northern Tasmania, Ricky scored several centuries and caught the eye of many scouts and companies.

His standout performances during this tour earned him a sponsorship deal with bat manufacturer Kookaburra. Ricky was only 12!

Much like his father, Ricky enjoyed playing Australian Rules Football and did so competitively until he was 14.

He decided to pack it in and concentrate on cricket after shattering his arm in a game. The fear that his next injury might ruin his chances of making it in cricket was a real concern, and Ricky made the mature decision to stop playing football.

Three years later, he signed with Tasmania and made his first-class debut in 1992 at 17. He performed well in his early years, but it took until 1995 for him to play his first ODI match. His Test debut followed quickly after in a home series against Sri Lanka, and with Ricky scoring 96 in his first innings, he was soon being talked about as the next big thing.

Ricky's first Test against England was even better. He scored a century and set in motion a period of dominance for Australia over England that had never been seen before. But Ricky's poor discipline and immaturity sometimes let him down, and he struggled with his fitness. This meant that he was in and out of the international setup quite a bit in his first years.

He got through that rocky patch and was soon a regular for Australia in both Test and ODI. His high scoring and passion made him a fan favourite, and he was named ODI captain in 2002. He followed this up with a star performance against England in the 2003 Ashes, as Australia pounded their old enemy 5–0.

That same year, Ricky and Australia won the 2003 Cricket World Cup, with Ricky batting 140 not out in the final. It was his first World Cup and Australia's second in a row. They would go on to win it again in 2007—this time with Ricky as captain—giving Australia an amazing treble. Their era of dominance was complete!

Although we remember Ricky Ponting as a superb batter, he was also recognised as one of the greatest fielders ever. His ability to catch when it seemed impossible led to many YouTube moments. Next time you are online, check some of them out!

Ricky continued playing at the highest level for a while longer, and by the time the 2011 World Cup came around, many people believed that Australia would make it four on the spin. They didn't, and a loss to India in the quarterfinals ended Australia's unbelievable run in World Cups. The defeat hurt, but we have to remember that India had players such as Sachin Tendulkar, MS Dhoni and Virat Kohli in their team that year, so there was no shame in losing to them!

Following the disappointment of the 2011 World Cup, Ricky gave up both the ODI and Test captaincy. He insisted he would keep playing for Australia if needed, but his performances had dropped a little by then. Pretty soon, the public was calling for him to be dropped altogether.

Ricky continued to play Test cricket for another year. Despite the criticism he had started to receive, he put in some amazing performances at times. In that period, he became only the third man to pass 13,000 career Test runs but decided to call it a day near the end of 2012.

Following his retirement from ODI and Test cricket, Ricky finished out the 2012–13 season with Tasmania, leading them to the 2013 Sheffield Shield championship. He was also the competition's leading run-scorer, with 911 (75.91 average). Seems like he was far from past it, despite what the critics had suggested.

Ricky has since moved into coaching. He took over at the Mumbai Indians in the IPL in 2014 and led them to the championship the following year. After that, he became coach of the Delhi Daredevils (now the Delhi Capitals), who had just finished last the previous season. He reshaped the team, brought through young players and changed the mindset of the whole franchise.

Ricky led them to top-three finishes every time in his first three years in charge of the Daredevils. He is still with the Capitals and desperate to win them their first-ever IPL championship. Having seen how often Ricky beat the odds in his playing career, we're willing to bet he will get them there!

CATHRYN FITZPATRICK

CAREER STATISTICS

	WTEST	WODI	WT20I	WLA
MATCHES	13	109	2	244
RUNS SCORED	152	651	–	1,970
BATTING AVERAGE	16.88	16.69	–	17.58
BALLS BOWLED	3,603	6,017	48	13,136
WICKETS	60	180	0	358
BOWLING AVERAGE	19.11	16.79	–	17.53

WTest = Women's Test cricket, WODI = Women's One Day International,
WT20I = Women's Twenty20 International, WLA = Women's List A cricket

BIOGRAPHY

Born	4 March 1968
Nationality	Australian
Test Debut	2 February 1991
Final Test	18 February 2006

Several times in this book, we've learned about female cricketers throughout history struggling to make a career in a sport they were so good at. Well, here is a woman who not only went through all of that discrimination but had to work two other jobs while she played cricket to pay the bills.

Cathryn Fitzpatrick worked as a waste collector and a postwoman while playing cricket for Australia, but that didn't stop her from becoming the fastest bowler in the history of the women's game. She terrorised batters for 16 years and helped to promote women's cricket all over the world.

Born on 4 March 1968 in Melbourne, Australia, Cathryn grew up knowing she had something different in her locker: an arm like a cannon. She would often play with the local boys' teams, and her bowling used to leave most of them open-mouthed. As a teenager, she continued to smash the stumps, hitting speeds with her bowling that seemed beyond belief.

By the time she was playing professionally, her ball speed was recorded at 75 miles per hour (125 kilometres per hour)!

Cathryn signed for the Victoria Women, a cricket team, in time for the 1989–90 season and won the Australian Women's Cricket Championships the following year. She went on to win it again in the 1995–96 season and then twice more in the early 2000s after it became the

Women's National Cricket League (WNCL).

Again, like Rachael Heyhoe Flint before her, Cathryn found the opportunity to play Test cricket scarce. She made her Test debut in 1991 and only ever got to play in 13 Test matches over the next 16 years. Still, she took 60 wickets in that time, putting her second on the Australian all-time list.

ODI matches were easier to come by. Rachael played in 109 of them throughout her career, taking a massive 180 wickets, a record that stood until 2017.

By 1997, she was seen as the most fearsome bowler in the history of the women's game. As that year's World Cup drew closer, a lot of fans expected Cathryn to lead Australia to glory. With the help of Belinda Clark and the rest of her teammates, she did just that, winning Australia's fourth (and Cathryn's first) World Cup.

Australia lost the final of the 2000 Women's World Cup to rivals New Zealand, so they came into the next one in 2005 dying to make things right. Their determination and skills were too much for the other nations, and Australia won a brilliant final against Mithali Raj's India.

Remember, Cathryn was achieving all this while working two other jobs. If that doesn't prove she is a superhero, then we don't know what will!

With her international career not beginning until she was 22, Cathryn didn't play at the top level for as long as some of her peers*. Players like Mithali Raj came into first-class cricket at 16, which gave them a lot more time to build up individual records. But Cathryn never seemed to let that bother her, and her devastating 75 miles per hour bowling took several decades to be equalled.

In 2006 and at the age of 37, she became the oldest woman in history to record a five-wicket haul in ODI history, and she announced her retirement from the game the following year. In her ODI career, she managed to become the first player to take over 100 wickets.

Cathryn also brought her domestic career to an end that year, finishing up with Victoria after 17 years of playing for them. In her time in the WNCL, she took 148 wickets in 103 matches.

She was named the head coach for the Australian team in 2012, and she led them through three hugely successful world championship campaigns before stepping down in 2015. Cathryn was inducted into the Australian Cricket Hall of Fame in 2019 and the ICC Cricket Hall of Fame the year after.

Cathryn Fitzpatrick might not have played for as long as some, but she still managed to win the lot. With her side jobs collecting waste and delivering the post, it's surprising that she found any time at all to play. Winning two World Cups in between all this is almost miraculous, and her aggressive bowling style has influenced many recent stars, including the likes of Lea Tahuhu.

Thankfully, the women's game is in better shape these days, but there is still more that could be done. Cathryn used to leave the boys in her neighbourhood in shock with her fast-paced bowling, so who is to say that she wouldn't have done the same at the top level if she'd been given more opportunities a little earlier in life?

... FINAL INNINGS

We hope that you enjoyed this book and that you learned something new about the players that we covered. It's never easy deciding who is the greatest, especially in a sport that has been around so long and has produced so many legends. Still, all we can do as fans is try!

Remember, the players on these pages haven't been numbered, so it is completely up to you to decide who is the GOAT. Maybe when you are next online, you can look up some of the older clips on YouTube and enjoy some classic moments. There are some beautiful cricketing clips out there if you search them up.

Of course, there won't be any footage of someone like Sir Jack Hobbs as he came along before cameras, TVs, social media, and, well, everything like that! But there is an endless stream of highlights from classic Ashes encounters and ODI battles, though. We do feel that reading about anything is always the best way to learn, but seeing it actually happen can bring home the sheer skill and emotions that were involved at the time.

Cricket has changed through the years, but not as much as other sports. Yes, we learned in this book that bowlers used to have to throw underarm and that there was a time when amateur cricket paid more than top-level cricket. Still, the fundamentals have remained basically the same. That is proof that cricket is a near-perfect sport, and all that we need to enjoy it is a ball, a bat, some stumps, and a group of people who want to play.

Like all sports, it takes different types of players to make it work. Some are more cautious and calculating, while others are all swashbuckling* style and aggression. Yet each individual can be legendary in their own way. It is the same in life in general. We can all excel at something, and we all eventually do. Don't ever think otherwise.

Players such as Virat Kohli and Belinda Clark were certainly born with something special, but they still had to work ridiculously hard to perfect those skills. Not much in this life comes easy, but it is the people who never give up that get to the top. Nothing is impossible, as you saw with W.G. Grace, who nearly died as a child when he contracted pneumonia, but still came through it to play top-level cricket into his sixties!

We must also remember that as the game progresses through time, so does the information on fitness, nutrition* and any number of things that can make a player better. The men and women who play today have better equipment, training and coaching, so the standard always rises. Saying that a player from 1922 wouldn't be as good in 2022 isn't a fair comparison, as the older player might have been even better with today's advantages, or they could have struggled against the higher quality all around them.

The same goes for any sport, really. Diego Maradona would surely have been even better in 2022 with all the protection players now get. He wouldn't be getting kicked 30 times a game. Boxers who fought 40 rounds until someone was knocked out back in the day would definitely have benefited throughout their career if they'd competed in the shorter, more controlled fights we see now.

But in truth, cricket is one of the sports with the least difference between then and now. Things have changed and improved massively, but someone like Brian Lara or Sir Viv Richards could have been the GOAT in any era; they were just that good. And that is why they have made this list.

So, we will end it there. As mentioned before, we hope that you had a good time reading up on some of the greatest cricketers ever to play the game. Remember to always try your best, do what's right and believe in yourself. That's what every player in here did, and they made it to the top. You can, too, in whatever you try if you give it your all!

GLOSSARY

Benedictine monks - Christian Brothers who follow St Benedict.

Bigwigs - The men and women at the very top, usually those with the money.

Bona fide - Genuine. The real thing.

Bumper contract - A highly paid contract.

Charisma - The ability to seem interesting to others. "Elvis Presley had real charisma on stage."

County cricket - Inter-county cricket matches. They have been played by counties in England and Wales as early as the 18th century.

East Zone - Cricket team that uses players from the eastern part of India.

Fast-tracked - Promoted quicker than normal.

First-class cricket - The highest form of cricket along with List A and Twenty20.

First Division - This was when the modern Premier League was called the First Division. It was the top division in English football.

Founded - To create or set up. It is usually used for sporting teams, franchises or businesses.

Fundamentals - The basics, but the most important parts, as the thing in question can't function without them.

Grassroots level - Building something from the bottom up. In terms of sport, it is the youth level.

Haul - To drag something. But in sport, it can mean a huge amount in scoring.

Latter - Comes after the former. Former means the first thing mentioned in a previous sentence, and the latter is the second.

Maiden - First.

Nutrition - The right foods we need to stay healthy.

Opportunistic - Someone who knows when to take an opportunity.

Out for a duck - Short for "Out for a duck's egg," which used to be said when a player was bowled out with zero runs. The zero on the scoreboard looked like a duck's egg!

Overwhelmed - When things become too much, or something or someone takes on too much.

Peer - A person who is on the same level as another in a place of work or in a sport.

Pioneering - A pioneer is the first to do something or someone who pushes for change.

Prestigious - High level or special.

Prodigy - Someone with exceptional skill in a sport, subject, etc.

Purple patch - A period when someone excels well above the norm.

Real estate - Collecting, selling or dealing with property such as houses.

Revolutionary - A complete change, usually for the better.

Sporadically - Here and there. Not consistently.

Stumping - When a fielder or wicketkeeper takes down the stumps to dismiss the batter.

Swansong - A final performance in someone's career.

Swashbuckling - Flashy, charismatic and cool.

Test cricket - The highest form of international cricket.

The Wanderers - An English football team that folded in 1887.

Trailblazer - Someone who creates their own path or a new style, etc.

U-boat - German submarines used in World War I and World War II.

UNICEF - The United Nations International Children's Emergency Fund. An organisation that helps those less fortunate.

Unorthodox - Not the norm. Different to what is expected.

Victorian - Usually the era in Britain during Queen Victoria's reign (20 June 1831 to 22 January 1901).

Wisden Cricketers' Almanack - An almanack is a yearly publication of lists, so the Wisden Cricketers' Almanack is a reference list of cricketers published in Britain each year.

Worrell Trophy - The Frank Worrell Trophy is a prize given to the winner of the West Indies versus Australia Test series.

Printed in Great Britain
by Amazon

25727035R00059